North American Indians Today

North American Indians Today

Apache

Cherokee

Cheyenne

Comanche

Creek

Crow

Huron

Iroquois

Navajo

Ojibwa

Osage

Potawatomi

Pueblo

Seminole

Sioux

North American
Indians Today

Osage

by
Philip Stewart

Mason Crest Publishers
Philadelphia

Special thanks to Robin Polhamus for her generous help writing this book.

Mason Crest Publishers Inc.
370 Reed Road
Broomall, Pennsylvania 19008
(866) MCP-BOOK (toll free)

First printing
1 2 3 4 5 6 7 8 9 10
Library of Congress Cataloging-in-Publication Data on file at the Library of Congress.
ISBN: 1-59084-674-5
1-59084-663-X (series)

Design by Lori Holland.
Composition by Bytheway Publishing Services, Binghamton, New York.
Cover design by Benjamin Stewart.
Printed and bound in the Hashemite Kingdom of Jordan.
Photography by Benjamin Stewart. Art on p. 6 by Keith Rosco. Artwork on pp. 26, 29, 30, 31, 32, 34, 55, 69, 74, 75 courtesy of Robin Polhamus.

Contents

Why is it so important that Indians be brought into the "mainstream" of American life?
I would not know how to interpret this phrase to my people.
The closest I would be able to come would be "a big wide river".
Am I then to tell my people that they are to be thrown into the big, wide river of the United States?

Earl Old Person
Blackfeet Tribal Chairman

Introduction

In the midst of twenty-first-century North America, how do the very first North Americans hold on to their unique cultural identity? At the same time, how do they adjust to the real demands of the modern world? Earl Old Person's quote on the opposite page expresses the difficulty of achieving this balance. Even the common values of the rest of North America—like fitting into the "mainstream"—may seem strange or undesireable to North American Indians. How can these groups of people thrive and prosper in the twenty-first century without losing their traditions, the ways of thinking and living that have been handed down to them by their ancestors? How can they keep from drowning in North America's "big, wide river"?

Thoughts from the Series Consultant

Each of the books in this series was written with the help of Native scholars and tribal leaders from the particular tribe. Based on oral histories as well as written documents, these books describe the current strategies of each Native nation to develop its economy while maintaining strong ties with its culture. As a result, you may find that these books read far differently from other books about Native Americans.

Over the past centuries, Native groups have faced increasing pressure to conform to the wishes of the governments that took their lands. Often brutally inhumane methods were implemented to change Native social systems. These books describe the ways that Native groups refused to be passive recipients of change, even in the face of these past atrocities. Heroic individuals worked to fit external changes into local conditions. This struggle continues today.

The legacy of the past still haunts the psyche of both Native and non-Native people of North America; hopefully, these books will help correct some misunderstandings. And even with the difficulties encountered by past and current Native leaders, Native nations continue to thrive. As this series illustrates, Native populations continue to increase—and they have clearly persevered against incredible odds. North American culture's big, wide river may be deep and cold—but Native Americans are good swimmers!

—*Martha McCollough*

Breaking Stereotypes

One way that some North Americans may "drown" Native culture is by using stereotypes to think about North American Indians. When we use stereotypes to think about a group of people, we assume things about them because of their race or cultural group. Instead of taking time to understand individual differences and situations, we lump together everyone in a certain group. In reality, though, every person is different. More than two million Native people live in North America, and they are as *diverse* as any other group. Each one is unique.

Even if we try hard to avoid stereotypes, however, it isn't always easy to know what words to use. Should we call the people who are native to North America Native Americans—or American Indians—or just Indians?

The word "Indian" probably comes from a mistake—when Christopher Columbus arrived in the New World, he thought he had reached India, so he called the people he found there Indians. Some people feel it doesn't make much sense to call Native Americans "Indians." (Suppose Columbus had thought he landed in China instead of India; would we today call Native people "Chinese"?) Other scholars disagree; for example, Russell Means, Native politician and activist, claims that the word "Indian" comes from Columbus saying the native people were *en Dios*—"in God," or naturally spiritual.

Many Canadians use the term "First Nations" to refer to the Native peoples who live there, and people in the United States usually speak of Native Americans. Most Native people we talked to while we were writing these books prefer the simple term "Indian"—or they would rather use the names of their tribes. (We have used the term "North American Indians" for our series to distinguish this group of people from the inhabitants of India.)

Even the definition of what makes a person "Indian" varies. The U.S. government recognizes certain groups as tribal nations (almost 500 in all). Each nation then decides how it will enroll people as members of that tribe. Tribes may require a particular amount of Indian blood, tribal membership of the father or the mother, or other *criteria*. Some enrolled tribal members who are legally "Indian" may not look Native at all; many have blond hair and blue eyes and others have clearly African features. At the same time, there are thousands of Native people whose tribes have not yet been officially recognized by the government.

We have done our best to write books that are as free from stereotypes as possible. But you as the reader also play a part. After reading one of these books, we hope you won't think: "The Cheyenne are all like this" or "Iroquois are all like that." Each person in this world is unique, whatever their culture. Stereotypes shut people's minds—but these books are intended to open your mind. North American Indians today have much wisdom and beauty to offer.

Some people consider American Indians to be a historical topic only, but Indians today are living, contributing members of North American society. The contributions of the various Indian cultures enrich our world—and North America would be a very different place without the Native people who live there. May they never be lost in North America's "big, wide river"!

The Osage have a long and proud history.

Chapter 1

History

Jesuit missionary and explorer Jacques Marquette first heard tales of the Wa-zha-zhe in 1673. The Illini Confederacy, a loose group of tribes in the northern Mississippi River valley, told him stories of a group of extremely large and fierce natives to the south. Following their directions, Marquette headed south and later that year established the first recorded contact with the Wa-zha-zhe in Vernon County, Missouri. The Frenchman wrote the name as "Ouchage," which the English would further distort into "Osage," the name by which they are known today. They in turn called the Europeans "Heavy Eyebrows," and the first Osage to encounter these outsiders found their body odor so revolting that it made some sick to their stomachs.

Traditions, language, and *archaeology* all link the Osage with the Dheigan-Sioux people, a group that would evolve into many of the tribes in the Central United States. Though these tribes were living on the Great Plains and along the Mississippi River at the time of the first European contact, they had migrated there from the valley of the Ohio River in the 1400s through the 1500s.

This group quickly split into various groups, among them the Osage, the

Little House on the Prairie

In *Little House on the Prairie*, by Laura Ingalls Wilder, the author recounts an encounter in 1870 with an Osage chief named Soldat du Chene (French for "Soldier of the Oak"). While it is possible Wilder got the name wrong, it appears quite evident from her description that she really did meet an Osage man. She noted his great height and unusual haircut. Some think that Osage hunting buffalo may well have set the prairie fires she records in the book.

Laura's family probably left their little house on the prairie because of an ongoing conflict with the Osage. A meeting was scheduled for August 1870 to resolve the situation between the Osage and the settlers, but was delayed until September so the Osage might complete their buffalo hunt. Most believed that either the Osage or the settlers would have to leave. The Ingalls family left just before the beginning of the meeting, no doubt thinking it would be the settlers who would have to leave. Instead, it was the Osage who were removed.

Omaha, the Ponca, and the Kaw. The Osage themselves continued this inclination toward disunity, splitting into various bands throughout their history. By the late 1700s, when contacts between the tribe and Europeans became more common, there were two established bands, the "Upper-Forest-Sitters," also known as the Big Osage, and the "Down-Below-People," sometimes known as the Little Osage. Sometime during the 1770s, a third group split from the Big Osage, moving south to become what was known as the Arkansas Band of Osage.

Despite these divisions, the groups maintained a common language and religion and remained in frequent contact with each other. They settled in southern Missouri and northwest Arkansas, though they frequently ranged further abroad to hunt or make war against other tribes. In fact, the Ute referred to them as *Com-an-te-che*, which means "those who want to fight all the time." (This same word was applied to the Comanche and was the origin of their name.) Other tribes were impressed by both their skill in battle and their great size: John Joseph Mathews noted that the average height for a male Osage was over six feet (1.8 meters), impressive today but even more impressive in an era when few men were taller than five feet nine inches.

The location of the Osage lands placed them at the junction between the three major *colonial* powers of North America: the French, the English, and the Spanish. The French, starting with Marquette, were able to establish trade and a loose alliance with the Osage, as did the Spanish to a lesser extent. However, no European nation was able to exert real control over the Osage, who continued to make occasional raids against both the Europeans and other tribes. The English never really achieved a peaceful coexistence with the Osage, in part because of the tribe's close relationship with the French, an enemy of the British.

Though the immediate effects on the tribe were small, the end of the eighteenth century saw claims to Osage lands change hands several times between the European powers. France sold the area, as part of the Louisiana Territory, to the Spanish, who later *ceded* it back to the French, who turned and almost immediately sold it to the young United States of America in 1803. Over the next few decades, the new nation managed to wrestle away much of the tribe's land through treaties, military force, and the sheer number of settlers to the area.

At about the same time, the area began to see an influx of settlers from other native tribes, such as the Cherokee, Fox, Sauk, Miami, and Kickapoo, pushed from their homes in the east by expanding populations of European settlers. The warlike and territorial Osage clashed frequently with these other tribes, particularly the populous Cherokee.

In 1808, under pressure from the federal government, the Osage ceded much of their lands to the United States, giving up more than half of the modern state of Missouri and much of northern Arkansas. The Osage moved to a *reservation* in southeastern Kansas, with a promise from the government that they would be left undisturbed by settlers and allowed to return to the old way of life. An 1824 act of Congress set aside roughly twelve million acres (4.9 million hectares) of land in southeastern Kansas for the tribe, but even there they would not remain undisturbed for long.

The return to the traditional way of life meant more than merely buffalo hunts. As the Osage asserted themselves in this new land, raids against other tribes resumed. A series of conflicts broke out, particularly against the Utes, Pawnees, Comanches, and Kiowas. These ended with a bloody raid against the Kiowa in 1833, which resulted in the massacre of 130 Kiowa women, children, and old men, and the theft of the *taime* medicine bundle, the Kiowa's most sacred religious artifact.

While the U.S. government had been largely content to let the Osage do

The Osage reservation.

as they pleased so long as they confined their attacks to Indians rather than settlers, the escalating war against the Kiowa was a great concern to federal officials. They worried that the violence might spill over into white settlements, and that the warlike Osage, *nominally* allies of the United States, might become difficult to contain and control, touching off violence across the western *frontier*.

In an effort to stop this progression of violence, Colonel Henry Dodge met with the Kiowa and agents of the Osage in the summer of 1834. Between them, they negotiated an end to hostilities between the tribes. Prisoners were returned, and the Kiowa chief Little Mountain traded his finest horse to Chief Clermont in exchange for the *taime*, without which the Kiowa were unable to conduct their annual **Sun Dance**. This agreement effectively marked the end of Osage raids against neighboring tribes.

In the following years, acts of Congress attempted to reshape the Osage lifestyle. Osage families were given **allotments** of land and encouraged to start farms. An 1839 agreement provided the Osages with cattle, hogs, plows, axes, a blacksmith, a miller, and farmers who would teach them farming methods. Although the Osage had planted corn, pumpkins, and gourds in their long-term camps, they were primarily **hunter–gatherers**, and reactions to the idea of farming generally ranged from *skepticism* to outrage. The few Osage who decided to try farming were condemned and threatened by their peers. The highly respected Chief George White Hair was told by his people that he would be removed from office if he persisted in farming. After much thought, White Hair slaughtered the animals, sold his farming implements, and held a huge feast, returning once again to the old life. His actions served to bring the Osage back together again, at least temporarily.

But the Civil War divided the Osage again, just as it did the rest of the United States. The **Confederacy** made arrangements for an alliance with the Osage, offering protection in exchange for a military post on the reservation and five hundred warriors for the Confederate Army. The Big Osage decided to fight with the Confederacy, but the men of the Little Osage fought on the side of the **Union**, despite the agreement. Both sides suffered greatly, not only in battle but also from the repeated raids by **guerilla** bands of white soldiers into Osage lands. Eventually, those Osage fighting for the Confederacy became discouraged by the lack of real leadership or protection, as well as the close proximity of Union troops. Only a few remained loyal to the Confederacy.

The Bureau of Indian Affairs had a role in Osage history and continues to be a part of the Osage's lives.

The Civil War had barely ended when the Osage found themselves once again under pressure to sell off more of their land. Americans scarred by the war were eager to start fresh lives in the West, and the Osage happened to be sitting on some of the finest farmland in the region. Over the objections of many Osage, four million acres (1.6 million hectares) on the northern and eastern sides of the reservation were sold in exchange for another promise that they would be left undisturbed by settlers on the remainder of the land. This promise lasted a mere three years before Congress attempted to buy the remainder of the land from the tribe. Under pressure from Samuel J. Crawford, the governor of Kansas (who was concerned the land would go to railroad companies instead of settlers), Congress ultimately rejected the plan, but the Osage's days on their Kansas reservation were numbered.

In 1869, an act was passed that allowed settlers to purchase lands from the Osage; in effect, this marked the end of the settlers' being kept out of the reservation. Crawford, well known for his dislike of Indians, did all he could to encourage settlers to move to the Osage lands. Hundreds of squatters—five hundred families according to Isaac Gibson, the Osage's government agent at the time—descended on the reservation.

In his annual report, Gibson states:

> Squatters have taken possession of the Osages' cornfields and forbid them from cutting firewood. . . . White men are constantly stealing or driving off their horses, over one hundred of their best horses stolen in the past month alone . . . scarcely a day goes by that they do not lose from five to twenty horses. They threaten to hang me, Crawford's men, if I interfere. . . . Which of these people are the savages?

Petitions and letters to Governor Crawford to stop the settlers, organized by a mixed-blood Osage named Augustus Captain, were met only with more federal encouragement to settlers. Angered by the continued petitions, Crawford asked the captain of a **vigilante posse** to shoot Augustus Captain, offering him a pardon if he did.

He never had the opportunity. No sooner had the governor acted than Gibson took the evidence he had gathered back to Washington and President Ulysses Grant. He negotiated another land exchange, this time with much better terms than Congress had offered before. Rather than the nineteen cents an acre offered in the 1868 plan, Gibson negotiated a price of

$1.25 per acre, a total price of over nine million dollars. Through the Osage Treaty of Stipulations Act of 1870, the government purchased the remaining eight million acres (3.3 million hectares) of Osage reservation land, holding the purchase price in the U.S. Treasury for the Osage. With the signing of the removal treaty, the Osage became America's wealthiest tribe.

The downside, of course, was that the Osage were now essentially homeless. They began searching for new lands with two criteria in mind.

Oil Boom Extravagance

Just like some lottery winners today, many Osage went on wild and irrational spending sprees with their new wealth. Grand pianos were purchased and left outside, year round. Expensive vases were used to store corn or vegetables. Some Osage bought shelves full of fine china and expensive kitchens, and yet cooked outside over a fire and ate with their fingers. One woman reportedly spent $40,000 in a single day for clothing, jewelry, and some land in Florida, sight unseen. Guardians sometimes built expensive houses for their charges . . . who then lived on the lawn in tepees.

Pawhuska was home to dealerships for all the most expensive manufacturers of automobiles in the 1920s, including Mercedes, BMW, and Pierce Arrow, the most expensive make of car at the time. According to one source, sparsely populated Osage County had more Pierce Arrows than any other county in the nation. While stories that suggest that some Osage would abandon cars rather than fill them with gas are probably exaggerations, other people tell stories of cars abandoned after even minor accidents.

Virtually all cars were black in those days or some other very dark color. Many Osage could not understand this and thought the dark colors boring. "They'd go to the dealership, find a car they liked, then point to a section of the blanket they were wearing and say 'Can I get it in this color?'" says Waltina Red Corn, an Osage elder. Since the Indians were more than willing to pay a premium for the outlandish colors, the dealers were happy to comply. "All over the rest of the country, the cars were black, but here we had all different colors, almost like a rainbow."

Heavy Eyebrows

While the eyebrows of the French were likely heavier than Natives' anyway, the difference was probably made even more striking by the grooming traditions of the Osage. The men of the tribe shaved their eyebrows, facial hair, and most of the head, leaving only a stripe about three inches (almost eight centimeters) wide and two inches (five centimeters) high down the middle of the scalp. Their bodies were covered with tattoos commemorating battles and hunts. It is little wonder the heavy-browed and frequently bearded Europeans were a shock to them. Likewise, the Europeans found the Osage men to be a frightening sight.

Meanwhile, the earliest accounts of the Osage women were not especially complimentary either: "Their personal appearance, with very few exceptions I can only specify three degrees: horrible, more horrible, most horrible," said Charles Joseph Latrobe, an early chronicler. It is likely, however, that this characterization was the result of the women's height and a few customs the Europeans must have found quite unusual. Osage women often powdered their bodies with a black powder made of dried plants and caked their faces with pumpkin pulp. The women, like the men, were often thoroughly tattooed as well. The result was an image that was probably at least as frightening as the Osage men. Whatever the reason for the Europeans' initial disapproval of the Osage women's appearances, they appear to have gotten over it fairly quickly, for by the end of the eighteenth century, intermarriage between Osage women and French traders had become quite common.

First, they wanted it to be located as near as possible to their ancient homeland in Missouri, so they might visit its sacred sites and burial mounds. The other was that it should be where they would never again be disturbed by white settlers. Many people among the tribe felt the only way to remain unmolested was to abandon their original lands and move to the far West, where they might resume the buffalo hunt and their old way of life.

One night, a tribal leader named Wah-ti-an-kah had a vision in his sleep of a land south of their Kansas reservation where his ancestors had once roamed—and where no white man would ever come to farm. Legend has it that he told his people there was something under the ground that would be very good for the Osage, a hint, perhaps of things to come. A group was sent to the south to investigate this land and found it just as he described it. It was mostly rocky hills, covered with tall grasses and scrubby forests. Buffalo herds still roamed the plains. No one would ever want to farm such land, but for hunters like the Osage, it was perfect.

There was just one problem: the Cherokee already owned the land. Gibson went to Washington to appeal to the government, and the result was the Osage Reservation Act of 1872, which legally affirmed the right of the Osage to the lands of Cherokee Outlet, as the area was known. The Cherokee were in some ways glad to get rid of the land. Many of the major livestock trails crossed the Outlet, and the animals frequently overgrazed parts of it. Timber thieves had made off with what little decent wood there was, and a recent government ruling had invalidated many of the Cherokee's grazing rights contracts with ranchers, significantly reducing what little income the Cherokee made from the land.

While the government paid for the purchase of part of the Cherokee Outlet, the Osage bought their portion outright, using some of the money from the sale of their old lands. The price, 70 cents an acre, seemed fair to some at the time, but history would prove this to be one of the nation's great real estate bargains. Since the Osage had purchased the land as its sole owners, they had more substantial legal claim on the land.

The Osage's new home was nearly one and a half million acres (about 202,000 hectares) on the eastern side of the old Cherokee Outlet. Of this, they sold 102,000 acres (about 41,000 hectares) on the western edge to their cousins, the Kaw. Much of the rest of the outlet was divided among other tribes the government had resettled, such as the Ponca, Tonkawa, Otoe-Missouri, and Pawnee.

Most Osage moved to this new land during 1871 and 1872. They seemed to be in a pretty good situation. The new land had cost significantly less than what they had received from the sale of their previous territory to the U.S. government, and the bulk of their nine million dollars still remained, accruing five percent annual interest in the federal treasury. The Osage also succeeded in striking several profitable deals with cattle ranchers, leasing out parts of the reservation for grazing.

But the good times were brief at best. Less than a year passed before the U.S. government began to again pressure the Osage to sell their land to settlers. This time, the Osage flatly refused. Because of the tribe's purchase of their new reservation land, the government had few legal means to remove the Indians, so it resorted to harsher tactics. Despite the enormous sum of Osage money in the Treasury, the treaties the tribe had signed never included any requirement for them to receive cash payments of the funds. Instead, the government had agreed to provide supplies such as food and medicine. In an effort to pressure the Osage to leave, the government arranged for these shipments to arrive late or spoiled. To make matters worse, **epidemics** of **smallpox**, **cholera**, and **tuberculosis** swept through the reservation. Alcoholism became a growing problem. By the mid-1870s, the buffalo herds were so depleted that the Osage were forced to return to farming, planting orchards, and growing vegetables and grain. At first, inexperience, a drought, and grasshopper infestation kept actual food production low. By 1875, merely half of the original Osage population remained.

But the tribe did not leave. For years, the tribe protested the government's decision to provide them with unusable supplies instead of cash. Finally, in 1879, a party of Osage led by Wah-ti-an-kah traveled to Washington to put an end to the situation. After a dramatic confrontation with the Commissioner of Indian Affairs, the federal government agreed to provide all the Osage's payments in cash, making them the first tribe to reach such an agreement.

Around the turn of the century, Congress passed the Dawes Act, which sought to end the traditional Native American practice of holding land in common to the entire tribe. Instead, the land was divided into allotments for each tribe member, and "surplus" lands were sold to settlers. In this way, the government sought to open up Indian lands to settlement and in the process, break down tribal social structures. Because they held **patented** title, the Osage should have been exempted from the provisions of the Dawes Act, but the government insisted on applying it to them anyway. In 1906, the Osage finally gave in, becoming the last tribe to undergo allotment.

Many of the tribe's records had been destroyed in a fire in 1893, so people of questionable heritage, the so-called "no-bloods," managed to sneak onto the roll. The tribal roll was determined to consist of 2,229 members, every child born before July 1, 1907. While those born after that date could still be considered tribe members, their "headright" to a portion of the tribal earnings would have to be inherited. Each Osage on the roll received allotments totaling just over a square mile (about 2.9 square kilometers), of which one 160-acre (65-hectare) section was designated as a homestead and exempted from taxation.

This old derrick and these graves are a memorial to Osage history.

In some ways, this was the beginning of a sad era for the tribe. Unfamiliar with the concepts and laws involved in land ownership, many Osage were swindled by crooked lawyers and bankers. For years, the government considered all Indians to be incapable of making legal and financial decisions themselves and appointed "guardians" to handle legal dealings for the full-bloods. Unfortunately, many of these guardians were corrupt and took advantage of their charges.

However, another major change was occurring in Osage country at about the same time. Oil had long been noted here and there around the region, in slicks on creeks and tarry springs. With a growing demand for petroleum, the potential of the Osage land became interesting to many **entrepreneurs**. The first oil lease, to a firm called the Indian Territory Illuminating Oil Company (ITIO), was signed in 1896. By the next year, the company had its first commercial well. Suffering from financial problems, the ITIO eventually subleased drilling sites to other companies, and the pace of exploration increased rapidly. In 1906, the Osage Nation's western lands were opened to oil exploration, while the ITIO retained rights to the east. Drilling continued to accelerate.

Little Las Vegas

At the height of the oil boom of the 1920s, the Osage were popular figures in some circles of high society. In the little town of Ralson, in Osage County, wealthy Osage took the idea of a speakeasy to the extreme. The operation was essentially a resort town, referred to as "Little Las Vegas." There was a beautiful swimming pool done in Mexican tile, gambling, canoeing, and feasting; alcohol and drugs flowed freely. The local law enforcement officers were paid to stay away, and Osage and their guests would party in high style with the elite of the day. There were thirty-six saloons—some elaborate establishments, others nothing more than tents. Hollywood celebrities would fly into Oklahoma especially to gamble and drink with the Osage. However, with the end of Prohibition and the oil boom, Little Las Vegas soon was no more.

In 1900, Osage County produced six thousand barrels of oil. Fourteen years later, it produced eleven million. Fueled by the growing American passion for the automobile and the demands of World War I, oil wells popped up all across the Osage lands. Because of the way they had purchased their land, the Osage, unlike many other tribes, retained full subsurface mineral rights to their land. Already wealthier than most tribes because of their funds in the U.S. Treasury and their grazing leases, the Osage were well on their way to becoming the richest group of people in the world.

Not everyone shared in the wealth. Many Osage were swindled out of headrights, and some, born after the deadline of the Allotment Act or living outside the reservation at the time, had no headrights to begin with. Soon, Osage society was divided into two distinct classes: the "haves" and the "have-nots." While many Osage were building huge houses and educating their children in the nation's finest universities, there were also those who lived in relative poverty. The gap between these groups, combined with the rough life common in **boomtowns**, made for a colorful but often dangerous situation in Osage territory.

Violence, alcohol, and prostitution were common in the Osage Nation. Police were often corrupt and little better than the criminals themselves. Towns were crowded with **speculators** hoping to strike it rich in the oil business. Housing was at a premium; people slept outside or in theatres and bars. Supplies were often lacking, and schools and doctors completely inadequate. Deadly fires, often resulting from accidents at oil wells, as well as explosions and tornadoes, devastated towns.

This period of lawless chaos hit its peak in the 1920s, during what some have called "the Reign of Terror." Beginning in 1921, at least twenty-four Osage, and probably considerably more, were murdered, often in schemes involving huge amounts of money or headrights. By some estimates, as many as sixty Osage, almost three percent of the tribe, were murdered in the early 1920s before law enforcement intervened in any meaningful way.

The more bountiful 1920s faded quickly, and the **Great Depression** did not spare the Osage. By the mid-1930s, control of much of the oil revenue had fallen into outside hands, and by 1935, less than a third of the original allotted lands were still owned by Osage. Many Osage who had left the reservation came back once they fell on hard times, in hopes that the bonds of tribe and family might earn them a little care there. Even those with headrights (called annuitants), however, suffered hard times as the Depression reduced demand for oil and revenues fell. Headrights, which had paid $15,000 a year in 1925, were yielding as little as $585 in 1932. In addition, the same terrible drought that affected the rest of Oklahoma dur-ing the 1930s hit Osage lands as well, and agriculture ground nearly to a halt.

Alcoholism had been a worrisome issue for many years, but during the 1930s it became more pronounced as poverty magnified the problem. **Pro-hibition** was **repealed** in 1933, and Congress ignored an appeal by the tribal council in 1934 to make alcohol illegal in Osage County. In addition, the new problem of drugs had begun to appear. A 1930 drug bust in Osage County proved the largest in state history until after the World War II. De-spite Prohibition, between 1930 and 1934 alone, forty-two Osage deaths were attributed to drugs or alcohol.

Recovery from the Depression was slow for many Osage. Government programs designed to spur economic improvement among Native Ameri-cans, such as the Indian New Deal, often specifically excluded the Osage, who were seen as wealthy despite the poverty some were suffering. Almost a third received no money at all from tribal sources. The tribe did manage

The sun rises over Osage land, bringing a new day of hope.

to obtain some relief through government grants and new oil and gas *royalties*, with which they created a health clinic, agricultural extension service, and an office of social services.

In the 1906 Allotment Act, the Osage Council was authorized until January 1, 1959. In 1957, Congress extended that deadline until 1984. About this time, discontent with the U.S. government began to grow among those without headrights who were not allowed to participate in the government. A group called the Osage Nation Organization was formed in 1964 to deal with this issue. Composed of both full-bloods and young, unallotted Osage of at least a quarter Osage blood, the group worked to increase the number of its members who could vote and to change the requirement that only full-bloods could serve on the council. The group had grown to eight hundred members by 1971, when a federal commission recommended that changes be made to the council. Despite this, no real changes were actually made.

Spurred by the Middle East oil *embargo*, oil revenues were once again booming by 1973. High prices and increased production raised headright income to almost $26,000 a year in 1980. The end of the embargo in 1983, however, triggered a steady fall in oil revenues for the Osage. While the effects of the crash are perhaps not quite as devastating as that of the 1930s, these have been hard times on the Osage reservation. Stores have closed, and people have moved away. Some buildings have begun to deteriorate.

Still, the Osage continue to remain hopeful. "There's a lot more to being Osage than just oil money," said a Hominy resident. "The Osage have seen a lot of ups and downs over the years. But they're still here." Strong family ties bind the tribe together, and it is this strong tribal identity, along with religious faith, that helps the Osage weather these tough times. An old Osage saying is "Nothing in the cosmos moves backward." The Osage view of the world has always been forward-looking, spurred by an undying hope for the future.

Artist Robin Polhamus's mural illustrates the Osage Creation story.

Chapter 2

Oral Traditions

Many Osage view the events of the preceding chapter as merely one part of their history; they consider their oral traditions to be another part that is equally as valuable. For centuries before Europeans began the written history of the tribe, the Osage told stories, some of them historical, some to explain natural phenomena, and others merely to entertain. Because there was no written form of the Osage tongue, these stories were passed down as oral traditions, told and retold from one generation to the next, sometimes changing slightly with each teller but still retaining the important heritage of the ancient past.

Many of the tribe's elders worry that the stories have been lost as the older tribe members have died. Some of those that survive, however, make a point of telling the stories they remember to today's children. Raymond and Waltina Red Corn, for example, invite children over to play in their tepee and listen to stories. While some stories may have been lost, many others will survive at least another generation, thanks to efforts like these.

The details of stories like these vary from place to place and family to family. No particular version is right or wrong.

Oral histories inspire contemporary artists with images from the Osage past.

Every group of people has its own version of the creation story, and few stories are as important. The creation **myth** is, in a way, at the foundation of every other story. It is the source of many of life's traditions and the basis for a people's view of who they are, and why they are here.

The Osage believe that the Children of the Middle Waters were sent by *Wah'kon-tah*, or God, to become caretakers of the Sacred One—the Earth. These people, who called themselves the Little Ones, floated down from the stars singly or in small groups, their legs stretched and their arms raised like the wings of a landing eagle. These movements are imitated in the creation dances. The Little Ones landed among the branches of a great red oak tree, shaking loose acorns that fell to the ground, and then they divided themselves into three groups. The People of the Water came first, then the People of the Land, and finally the People of the Sky.

Before they left the Sky Lodge, their grandfather the Sun called them to him and asked them to notice the thirteen rays that shone from him during certain conditions. These rays were perfectly straight; six streamed out of his left side and seven from his right side. On the left shone a soft glow, like the under tail feather of a golden eagle. These things, warned the Sun, would have great significance in their coming lives upon the Sacred One.

At night, the people sat around the campfire and looked up at the stars, their brothers who had remained in the sky. The people learned their brothers' positions and seasonal movements.

One day, while the three groups were traveling, the Water People went out ahead, while the Land People and the Sky People fell behind. The Water People came to a river, which was happily singing and whispering between the rocks while the trees listened intently to its song. As the Water

Robin Polhamus's artwork recreates the Osage past.

People stood listening as well, their leader saw a man standing in the middle of the water.

The leader knew instantly who this was. He turned to his people and said: "Here stands *Wah-sha-she*, whose body is the waters of the earth." The river spoke to the Water People through Wah-sha-she.

"Oh, Little Ones," said the river, "if you make your body of me it will be difficult for death to overtake you, and you will make clean all that comes to you."

The leader discussed this with his people, and they all agreed that from then on they would be known as Wah-sha-she, the Name Givers, for the river had given them his name, and they would from then on represent all the waters of the earth. The Name Givers then named the Land People *Hunkah*, which was the name of the Sacred One. Then they named the Sky

The village of the Isolated Earth People, as portrayed by Robin Polhamus.

The Isolated Earth People joined with the others to become one people.

People, calling them *Tzi-Sho*, after the Sky Lodge from which they had come.

The people were pleased to have their names, but they knew they were not whole, for they had been told to find the group of people who were native to the earth, called the *U-tah-non-dsi*, the Isolated Earth People. Once they found this group, they would be a complete clan, symbolizing within their group the entire cosmos. They set out again, this time to find the Isolated Earth People.

Finally, the Water People came to a village. The three groups were afraid to approach the settlement, so they sent a messenger instead. He climbed the ridge above the village, where he hid himself. The smells of the village below rose up into his nostrils, so terrible they made him sick.

The people he saw were strange to him. The men had bangs and were tattooed around the lips and eyes. The women wore only deerskin aprons

Oral traditions were passed from generation to generation.

and robes, which they let slide from their shoulders. The girls walked in pairs, followed by groups of young men, who acted like dogs or coyotes. The girls would throw rocks at the boys, who would dodge them, and then the girls rushed the boys, snarling and growling like she-wolves.

The messenger had seen enough. He went back to his people and told them he had found the village of the Isolated Earth People. The leader of the Water People went forward to meet the leader of this strange people, but the Land People and Sky People could not stand the smell and walked off, holding their noses. As the Water People's leader came closer to the village, he saw the bones of men and animals scattered about, while wolves and coyotes laid in wait, and vultures circled overhead, drawn by the scent of decay.

At the edge of the village, two men were fighting with clubs, while a man in women's clothing ran away in fear. The Water People's leader could see a man lying dead in a lodge, while his brother stood above him, wiping the blood from his war club. All around was death, disease, and decay, which was what would be expected of earth, without the influence of the sky.

The chief of the Isolated Earth People sent out a messenger of his own, who asked the leader of the Water People to come to the village to smoke the pipe with their chief. Once they had passed the pipe between them, the leader of the Water People asked the other chief, "Who are you?"

The chief replied, "I am of the earth people and the red boulder is our symbol. It is red like the dawn and it is life everlasting. When they come to it, the enemy war parties must divide and pass on each side; all things move aside for the great red boulder."

The leader of the Water People then said, "Our bodies are of the red clay, like the pipe we are smoking. We are the Wah-sha-she, the Water People, and all things come to us for purification."

The chief of the Isolated Earth People listened long to the wisdom of

The Osage people keep the past alive even while embracing the twenty-first century.

Traditional Osage dress, portrayed by Robin Polhamus.

Water People's leader. He soon decided that his people would move away from their village and join with the Children of the Middle Waters, to become one people, representing the whole world: Sky, Earth, Land, and Water. (Two more clans, called "The Last to Come," would later join the Osage as well, becoming part of the Sky People.)

This was the beginning of an age of great plenty and happiness. There was always more than enough meat, and no enemies troubled them. However, as time passed, the old men became appalled with the ways of the tribe's youth. They thought the energy of the young was better put to other purposes. These old men began to meet under the shade of an elm tree, where they would sit all day and smoke with Wah'kon-tah (God), moving each day a little further from the village to escape the distractions and noises.

Together, these old men began to lay the foundations of their culture. They created an organized religion, the buffalo hunt, a war movement, and a civil government. Because of this, they were called the Little Old Men, or the wise men.

After they had met under the elms for a long while, a man offered them the use of his lodge. Soon, to the donor's great pleasure, it became known as the Lodge of Mystery. After a long while, the Little Old Men, because of their closeness to Wah'kon-tah, became holy, and likewise the lodge too became holy. They began their recitations with these words: "It has been said in this lodge."

As they talked among themselves, the Little Old Men began to worry that the Isolated Earth People, now a division of what was called the Grand Hunkah, was not being influenced enough by the other divisions, the Land

The clan system of the Osage is extremely complex, with a web of subdivisions and multiple symbols. The relationship between the clan and the life symbol is frequently misunderstood, even by some members of the tribe. Although each clan had a life symbol, the clans did not have particular names and most were referred to by a wide range of terms that had either a direct or symbolic connection to that symbol. Some legends refer to the life symbol as an ancestor, or use terms like "grandfather" or "grandmother," but these were merely terms of respect, not strictly meant to indicate an actual biological relationship. According to one Osage, "We do not believe that our ancestors were really animals, birds, etc., as told in the traditions. These are only *wa-we'-ku-ska-ye*, symbols of something higher."

In the ancient rituals, members of the clans spoke of having "taken for their body" the symbols. According to Francis LaFlesche, this phrase meant that from the symbols they would "receive the means by which to sustain and prolong life." Each symbol had some admirable quality that, if humans could attain it, could help them in life. For example, hawks, bears, and pumas had great courage, while otters and beavers were great swimmers. Even the freshwater mussel had something of value: its long life.

> The distinction between the people of the *Tzi-Sho*, or Sky People, and those of the Grand *Hunkah*, or Earth People, was a central one to many aspects of traditional Osage life. Villages were laid out along a central east–west road. The Sky People lived to the north of this dividing road, the Earth people to the south. The Peace Chief was always a member of the Sky People, while the War Chief was chosen from among the Earth People.
>
> This division also regulated marriage. Members of the Sky People were required to marry those from the Earth People, and vice versa. Thus, every Osage child was, in fact, the product of a union between the entire universe, earth and sky.

People and the Water People. The old men were concerned that the Isolated Earth People might return to their old ways.

So the Little Old Men decided they would divide the four groups into twenty-two original *gens*, each of which would have its own sub-gens. Each gen would choose a living symbol to honor. There were so many gens that practically every single thing in nature with any desirable characteristics would be picked by someone.

The Little Old Men sent out all the men to *fast*, wearing a sacred earth mark on their foreheads. When they returned, they told the Little Old Men their experiences and visions, and from this could be determined a sign from Wah'kon-tah as to what their life symbol was to be.

At last, it seemed all the honorable symbols had been chosen, and only one man from the Isolated Earth People was left without a life symbol. Frustrated, he went out again to find his symbol. While he was traveling, he accidentally walked into the web of a black spider. He was annoyed and asked the spider, "Why did you build your web here, where I would walk into it?"

The spider replied, "Why don't you choose me as your life symbol?" The man stifled a laugh with his hand, but the spider said, "Don't laugh. You came to me, and where I build my home, all good things come to me."

In the first days, when the Osage were beginning to descend from the sky, they found that the land was completely covered in water. They floated about, looking for somewhere to land. The people called for the Elk, who was the most impressive of all the animals, inspiring confidence in everyone.

The Elk went down into the waters, but despite his confidence, he began to sink. He called out to the Great Winds for help. The Winds rose up from the four directions of the Earth, gathering up some of the water and carrying it up to the sky in the form of mist.

At first only a few rocks were exposed, but eventually more and more land began to appear—but there was still nothing for the Osage to eat. The Elk was so overjoyed with what he had done, however, that he began to roll over and over on the new, fertile ground. As he rolled, loose hairs from his coat became lodged in the wet ground. Amazingly, the hairs began to grow; the first became beans, corn, potatoes, and wild turnips. Then still more hairs became the grasses of the plains, and finally the great trees of the forest.

One day, a young Osage named Little One began to contemplate the nature of life. *Why is it that people must grow old and die?* he asked himself. *What is the meaning of life?* No matter how long he thought, he could not seem to come up with satisfactory answers to these questions.

He went to the elders and asked them these questions. The elders all tried to answer, but their replies did not satisfy him either. Finally, he realized that only one thing was left for him to do. He would have to seek his answers in dreams.

So he arose early in the morning and prayed to Wah-kon-tah for assistance. Then he turned and walked from the village, taking nothing with him, not even food or water. He traveled over the plains and into the hills looking for a place far away from his people, where no one would disturb him. This was the sort of place he needed for a vision to come to him.

He walked for many days. Every night he camped in a different place, hoping that each place would be the right location to give him the dream he wanted. But no dreams came. At last he came to a hill that rose above the surrounding landscape like the curved breast of a turkey. A huge elm tree grew on the slope, and near its base a spring poured forth. Little One was so impressed by the beauty of the place that he was sure the power of Wah-kon-tah filled it. He decided to make his camp there. Leaning against the base of the tree, he sat back and waited for the sun to set. Soon he drifted off to sleep, but no signs came to him.

When he woke up the next morning, he found himself faint with hunger. The days without food had taken their toll. *I must go back home,* he thought. He thought of his family and realized he had been gone a long time. While it was not unusual for a man to seek wisdom in this way, he knew they would be concerned. *If I do not turn back now, while I still have a little strength left,* he thought, *I will die out here, and my family will never find my body.*

He began to follow the stream that ran from the spring, down the hill toward his village. He walked and walked until he was nearly home. Suddenly, he caught his foot on the tangled roots of an old willow that grew near the banks of the stream. By this time, he was so weak that he was unable to rise, so he merely lay there, clutching the willow's roots.

"Grandfather," he said to the ancient willow, "I can't go on."

Then the old tree spoke. "Little One," it said, "all the people cling to me for support as they walk along life's path. Look at the base of my trunk, which sends out the roots that anchor me to the ground. They show my age. They are blackened and wrinkled, but they remain strong. That strength comes from relying on the earth. When people use me as a symbol, they too will live to grow old as they travel the path of life."

The willow's words strengthened Little One. He stood up and began to walk again. When he caught sight of his village at last, he sat down in the grass to rest a moment. And then finally, as he sat looking at his village, a vision came to him. An old man approached Little One in his dream. Little One did not think he had ever seen the man before, but he looked strangely familiar, nonetheless.

"Look upon me," the old man said to him. "What do you see?"

"I see an old man," said Little One, "his face wrinkled with age."

"Look upon me again," said the old man.

Then Little One looked harder, and as he looked, he was reminded of what the willow had told him. "I see an old man in sacred clothing," he said. "The fluttering down of the eagle adorns his head. It is you, my grandfather. I see an old man with a pipe in his mouth. I see you, my grandfather. You are strong and rooted to the earth like the willow. I see you standing among the day of peace and beauty. I see you, my grandfather. I see you standing as you will stand in your lodge."

The old man smiled, for Little One had seen things truly. "My young brother," he said, "your mind is fixed upon the days of peace and beauty." And then he disappeared.

Little One found himself full of peace, and when he returned to the village, he was no longer troubled by the questions that had driven him on his quest. He realized the old man he had seen was in fact himself. The man in his vision was the elder he himself would one day become, filled with peace and wisdom and strength for his people.

From then on, he began to listen more carefully to the words of his elders, and he spent more time among them. And from that day forward, of all the young men of the village, he was by far the happiest.

These are just a few of the stories told by the Osage over the years. No matter what the stories' origins, they have survived the centuries because they fill a certain need. Whether that need is to teach, amuse, or comfort, they form an important backdrop to the lives of modern Osage, and they will no doubt continue to be passed down through families for years to come.

The Osage Nation tribal seal.

Chapter 3

Current Government

"Tribes are not only cultural and ethnic entities, but also political entities, recognized as foreign governments by the federal government under the commerce clause," says Joe Conner, who sometimes teaches classes on tribal government. And yet, tribes are also part of the United States. This seeming contradiction has led to a long history of conflict and confusion between the two governments. Tribes establish social programs, levy their own taxes, and can be immune to state laws and taxes.

For the Osage, the tribal government takes on particular importance because of its management of the reservation's mineral rights, particularly the tribe's vast reserves of oil and gas, the rights to which are leased to outside companies. This amounts to millions of dollars worth of resources. The role of the council is not only that of a local government; council leaders must also be able to run a profitable business.

The primary organization of the Osage tribal government is the Osage Tribal Council, which is in fact run very much like a corporate board of directors, acting without a **constitution** or **charter**. In addition to this council, there are lesser councils elected to represent the interests of each of the three primary villages of the Osage and to report to the tribal council.

The tribal council consists of a principal chief, an assistant chief, and eight council members, all elected by popular vote to terms of four years. However, only those tribal members who possess headrights can vote in the elections. Their vote counts according to the proportion of their headrights; the more headrights, the more their individual vote counts. This has long been a point of contention, because a significant number of Osage, nearly 13,000 of the 17,000 registered tribe members, have no headrights. Because of this, a majority of tribe members have absolutely no say in their tribe's government.

The current situation, with its system of voting by headright, was created by an act of Congress in 1906. Besides setting up a tribal government to administer the mineral estate of the tribe, this same act also assigned allotments and headrights to each Osage, with which came the right to vote in tribal elections. This new system effectively replaced the previous government, which had been disbanded in 1900 by the Secretary of the Interior. This earlier government, established by an 1881 constitution, had been open to participation by all members of the tribe and was closely modeled on the U.S. government.

In 1991, a group of Osage filed suit in federal court challenging the validity of the restriction on voting rights. They hoped that the court would uphold the 1881 constitution and allow for the reestablishment of tribe-wide voting rights. Instead of directly settling the issue, however, the court ordered the creation of a constitutional commission to study a reworking of the Osage government, an expansion of voting rights to all *lineal descen-*

The Osage city of Hominy has its own public services.

Robin Polhamus's mural of Creation is in the Osage tribal council's.

dants of the original tribal roll, and an eventual **referendum** on a new Osage constitution.

The court-ordered referendum occurred in 1993, and voters chose to support a government in which all Osage would have the right to vote on a government that was in charge of non-mineral issues. This would be known as the Osage National Council and was modeled after the U.S. government. This council would be led by a president, vice president, and a legislature, as well as a newly created courts system headed by an elected judge. Meanwhile, the mineral resources would continue to be regulated by a separate council—the Osage Tribal Council—whose members would be elected by headright holders only.

Elections were held for both councils in 1994. However, no sooner had the elected council members taken office, than the Osage Tribal Council filed an appeal with the Tenth Circuit Court of Appeals in Denver contending that the new government was illegal. In 1997, the court ruled, reversed the earlier decision, and reinstated the Osage Tribal Council as the sole ruling body of the tribe. They found that the 1991 court decision was beyond the jurisdiction of the court and contradicted both an act of Congress and the earlier **precedent** set by the U.S. Supreme Court.

The Osage Tribal Administration Building.

Some Osage saw this as a victory for tribal **sovereignty**, supporting the right of tribes, as sovereign nations, to enter into agreements with Congress. Others saw it as a defeat for the principle of democracy.

The decision created a great deal of hard feelings, particularly among Osage without a share in the mineral estate. Some claim that the wording of the 1906 Allotment Act, which the Supreme Court upheld, indicates that the trust responsibility of the government to the tribe lasts only as long as

Native America

The thirty-nine recognized tribes of Oklahoma have more than 400,000 registered members, and many more Oklahomans claim some degree of native ancestry. Between them, these tribes employ 15,000 people, making them the state's fourth largest employer. "If you've got something bad to say about Indians, you better be careful what you say in Oklahoma," says Brite Starr. "Because the odds are pretty good you're talking to one."

members of the tribal roll are still live. They also point out that the Allotment Act provides no means for establishing a new roll, which had been one of the goals of the Osage National Council. If this were true, then with the death of the last of the original allotees, the trust responsibility would end. It is not clear under the 1906 legislation whether the act gives the tribal council outlined there the responsibility for anything but administering the mineral estate and division of land. Raymond Theis II, Second Speaker of the Osage National Council, points out: "It does not say anywhere in the 1906 act that the tribal council can carry out other duties. So what they are attempting to do has no basis under this act."

For now, the tribe seems to have settled back into having one council, but it is unlikely that the last of this issue has been heard. Members of the Osage National Council have been appealing to their elected representatives in the federal government, and many Osage still support a change in tribal government.

Despite the controversy, the Tribal Council has made assurances that

Chief Charles O. Tillman and his wife Julia.

Osage Nation membership cards.

Governor Joe was an early leader of his people. He negotiated and signed the deed with the Cherokee for the land that is now the Osage Reservation.

The state's license plate shows an Osage shield of buffalo hide, crossed with a peace pipe and an olive branch, Indian and European symbols for peace.

they will keep in mind the interests of all Osage, not just those with a share of the mineral rights. The tribal government does provide a number of services for tribe members, both with tribal funds and with the administration of federal funds.

Social services offer a range of programs similar to those offered by many state governments. For example, Child Protective Services and Indian Child Welfare work to prevent the abuse and neglect of children, while strengthening family structures. A foster care program provides short-term accommodations for children in difficult situations. Other programs provide financial support for those who cannot afford basic living needs. Some of these programs, such as the Low Income Energy Assistance Program, which provides winter heating and summer cooling assistance for low-income Osage, are funded by the federal government. Educational programs provide scholarship assistance for Osage students seeking to attend college or obtain vocational training. The Academic Achievement Scholarship, for instance, is designed to encourage Osage college students to excel, by providing a reward of one hundred dollars each semester they attain a grade point average (GPA) of 3.25 or above.

While many Osage seem to feel that their government is doing a fairly good job administering these programs, tribal politics are likely to continue to be every bit as **contentious** as national politics, perhaps more so. The community is small, and most people are related somehow, so political infighting can get particularly nasty. "Some people don't realize we've got much more conflict within our own government than we ever had with the United States," says Buddy Red Corn.

Osage spirituality is closely connected to the natural world.

Chapter 4

Modern Religion

Sunlight streams through the intricate artwork of the stained glass windows, making the inside of the church glow with a soft radiance. Some windows depict scenes from the Bible, familiar to most. Other images are less familiar. It is a setting worthy of the world's great cathedrals, and indeed, the windows were fashioned by some of Europe's finest craftsmen—but the church is in Pawhuska, Oklahoma, not Paris, Munich, or Rome. In addition to the biblical stories familiar to Christians, one also sees in the stained glass Native Americans, some recognizably Osage.

The Immaculate Conception Catholic Church stands as testament not only to the considerable influence of the Catholic Church on the tribe but to the important place spirituality has in Osage society. This faith comes in many forms, but few Osage do not claim some sort of religious affiliation, and there are many that mingle both old and new ways.

From the very beginning, the Osage were one of the most profoundly spiritual tribes. In every aspect of life—hunting, farming, war, peace, childhood, birth, and death and everything in between—Osage life was saturated with ritual. Even closely related tribes were amazed at the extent of Osage religion. A young member of the Omaha, a tribe so closely related to

A plaque commemorates the centennial of the Kaw's gift of the I'n-lon-schka to the Osage.

the Osage that they spoke nearly the same language, commented on a visit he made to the Osage in the 1870s:

> Before sunrise in the morning following the first night of our visit, I was awakened by the noise of a great wailing. I arose and went out. As far as I could see men, women, and children were standing in front of their houses weeping. My parents explained to me that it was the custom of the [Osage] people to cry to *Wa-kon-da* morning, noon, and evening. When I understood the meaning of the cry I soon learned not to be startled by the noise.

Traditional Osage religion was also extraordinarily complex. In general, priesthoods could be broken into four general classes: the clan priests, also known as the *non-hon-zhin-ga* ("Little Old Men"), the *Wa-wathon* priests or *ni'-ka don-he* ("Good Men"), the Great Bundle priest or *ton' won a-don-be* ("Village Guardian"), and the Great Medicine Bundle priest. The clan priests were responsible for rituals concerning the visible world, such as war, hunting, weather, and child naming. The Wa-wathon priests conducted the peace ceremony, while the Great Bundle priest dealt with the New Year rite and the tattooing ceremonies. The responsibilities of the Great Medicine Bundle priest are unclear, but seem to have involved healing and health-related rituals.

Within the clan priests, alone, there were twenty-four different priesthoods, one for each clan. These, in turn, had seven different degrees of initiation through which a priest had to progress, each with its own rituals and responsibilities. There were also dozens, probably hundreds, of special ritual objects, called *wa-xo'-be*, most of them specially constructed

Some worship at the "indoor church" at Osage Indian Baptist Church.

bundles of certain elements, each with its own particular role in Osage ritual.

Sadly, much of the Osage religion has been lost today. The repeated re-settling of the tribe, along with the drastic drop in their population following their move to Oklahoma (from 3,700 in 1872 to less than a thousand twenty years later) so thoroughly disturbed the complicated structures of clans and priesthoods that the religion was fatally disrupted. Often the priests of the proper authority for a particular ritual were unavailable, and when the last of a particular priesthood died out, there was no one left to train a replacement.

By the 1880s, this had left a void in the lives of the normally religious Osage. The loss became particularly painful as the tribe sought order and moral structure during the lawless and chaotic days of the oil boom.

Tribe members filled this void in different ways. The Catholic Church had been active among the tribe for years, beginning with Marquette's first meeting with the tribe, and it had won a few converts over the years. The *Jesuit* priests were always welcome among the Osage and won great respect for their help during the smallpox and measles epidemics. But a bad experience with Presbyterian missionaries left the Osage very skeptical about the Protestant faith.

In 1847, the Catholic Church founded a mission and school for Osage living on the Kansas reservation. Mother Bridget Hayden and Father John Schoenmakers, both stationed at the mission, are important figures for the Osage; they not only taught the Osage about religion, but they also estab-

An indoor shelter for the I'n-lon-schka dance ceremony.

The Osage gather here to be part of the I'n-lon-schka.

lished the first schools for the tribe. With the loss of the traditional religion the Osage, who had always welcomed the Catholics into their communities, became more involved in the church. Today most Osage consider themselves Catholic.

A few lines from "The Songs of the Waters," the fifth part of "The Songs of *Wa-xo'-be*":

Wa-kon-da, thou holy one, permit us to cross this water,
Permit us to cross, permit us to cross,
Thou wingless one, thou who art our grandfather.
Wa-kon-da, thou holy one, permit us to cross this water,
Permit us to cross, permit us to cross,
Thou Sacred Beaver, thou who art our grandfather.
Wa-kon-da, thou holy one, permit us to cross this water,
Permit us to cross, permit us to cross,
Thou Great Otter, thou who art our grandfather.
Wa-kon-da, thou holy one, permit us to cross this water,
Permit us to cross, permit us to cross,
Thou Great Puma, thou who art our grandfather.

Looking up through the I'n-lon-schka bell tower.

Osage women take much pride in dressing their husbands, sons, and daughters for the ceremonial dance. Robin Polhamus portray's the wife of Blue Mark Starr getting him ready for the I'n-lon-schka.

Some Osage are also members of Protestant churches. The Osage Indian Baptist Church in Pawhuska is one such congregation. Similar in many respects to the Southern Baptists, the church is modest but welcoming, founded on allotted land donated by the Strike Axe family. The church still receives money each quarter from a fraction of a headright donated by an allotee whose will divided his headright equally between his twenty-nine cousins and the church.

Today, the church is not much different from your average American Baptist church, though the occasional ponytail on the men or the beadwork on the older members' clothing suggests their native heritage. Older members still recall the way it was in earlier times. "I remember when you'd look over this room, and all you'd see was folks in blankets," says

WERE OPPRESSED. (ACTS.10.38)

IN MEMORY OF
JOSEPH BUFFALOHIDE.

The Cathedral of the Osage

The Immaculate Conception Catholic Church, located in the Osage capitol of Pawhuska, seems strangely out of place in the small country town. Begun in 1910, the French Gothic structure was funded largely by donations from the tribe's booming oil revenues. The building itself is impressive, but by far the most notable feature is the twenty stained glass windows. Created by some of Europe's most skilled craftsmen, the windows were sent from Munich, Germany, accompanied by the artisans who installed them.

While many windows depict Bible stories, there are others that show scenes of particular importance to the Osage. In one scene, Christ is seen speaking to the Osage children; in another we see Columbus's first meeting with the Indians. Permission was attained from the Vatican in 1919 to depict living persons in the windows, and careful inspection shows recognizable figures from the local community, such as Father John Schoenmakers, from the Catholic mission, and several prominent Osage.

Stained glass windows carry their own message of spirituality to the Osage people.

Cedar

An important element in many Osage traditions is the smoke from burning cedar wood, which is considered a form of purification. Many ceremonies call for washing one's hands and then being exposed to cedar smoke. It is important that things be done in that order, since by washing afterward one might nullify the cleansing effects of the smoke. When a member of the drum committee dies, the drum, said to be in mourning, is smoked with cedar by an elder. (The drum is not burned, but the sweet-smelling cedar smoke is wafted around it.)

The reason behind the tradition lies in the nature of the cedar tree itself. The Osage revered the cedar tree because, unlike the other trees, it appeared alive all year-round. Its gnarled roots and drooping branches reminded them of the toes and bent shoulders of the elderly, and thus the cedar became a symbol of long life, and its fragrance signified great power. In Osage legend, the Tree of Life is a female cedar, growing by the River of Life in an Eden-like garden.

Raymond Red Corn, perhaps the tribe's oldest living half-blood, referring to the traditional blankets the Osage wore during the winter or for special occasions. The congregation is small, but the people are committed to their church, and the pastor, Creth Hopkins, is hopeful about the future. He points to the increased involvement of families in recent days. "Look at the number of men here today," he says, indicating the dozen or more present. "We used to only have a handful here on Sundays, now look how many more there are."

By the 1880s, several religious movements of Native origin rather than European had also begun to spread among the American tribes. The first, the Ghost Dance, was brought to the Osage by Sitting Bull, an Arapaho. It was performed only once, and the Osage mostly rejected it, disappointed by the failure of a prophet to appear as promised. A similar faith, taught by Otoe prophet William Faw Faw, reached the Osage in 1894 or 1895. Although it was met with more acceptance than the Ghost Dance, Old Man Faw Faw's Dance, as it was called, did not create a lasting impact on the Osage either.

The movement that did attract many Osage adherents was peyotism, in the form of the Native American Church. While the exact origins of the faith are unknown, it may have originated in the Carrizo culture of Texas. The Native American Church combines traditional beliefs and the use of the *hallucinogenic* plant peyote with Christian beliefs. Introduced to the Osage in 1898 by John Wilson, a Caddo/Delaware, the new religion quickly won many converts. By 1910, it had largely supplanted the traditional religion.

The Native American Church continues among the Osage today, although their numbers are considerably reduced. In 1980, there were fewer than 150 active members. Because of public perception of peyote use, the

---

Osage Names

Within the original Osage society, children had two names—one they had when they were young and a second they received when they were older. Young children were often called by nicknames or names meaning only "first son" or "second son," and so on. Today, children are given English names at birth. But at some point, usually upon reaching puberty, they receive an Osage name in the traditional ceremony.

This ceremony, like many others, involves a meal prepared for the guests. An elder conducts the ceremony, smoking the person with cedar smoke, and presents the youth with the chosen name. Names are chosen to suit the person, but are also influenced by the person's clan affiliation. Names of people from the Sky Clans, for instance, include such meanings as "Hawk That Flies Before the Storm" or "Little Cloud That Floats Alone."

Naming is important because it signifies acceptance by the tribe as an adult. Originally, only boys were named, but the tradition has been extended to girls as well. Only those who have undergone the naming ceremony are allowed to dance in the I'n-lon-schka.

Osage life was once filled with a sense of the spiritual world. Today, many Osage are recapturing that awareness. Something as ordinary as the sun rising over their land may carry spiritual messages.

church maintains a fairly low profile, though the courts have upheld the legality of their practices.

Peyote is consumed as a **sacrament** at several points in all-night **vigils** and generally not in such a way that it causes visions. The cactus is considered a gift from God to promote health and righteousness. Much of the time at church meetings is spent singing. Unlike many religions, the church has no professional clergy, and members are free to interpret the Bible's teachings as they see fit. The moral code is mostly Judeo-Christian, with special emphasis placed on abstaining from alcohol and remaining faithful to one's spouse.

Osage participants in Catholic, Protestant, and Native American Churches, as well as those of no particular organized faith, all have one common link: the *I'n-lon-schka*. Most Osage, regardless of other affiliations, are involved to at least some degree in the annual festival. The I'n-lon-schka is one of the few authentic tribal dance festivals still performed regularly in the United States, though it is not strictly an Osage ritual.

While parts may be closely related to ceremonies of the traditional Osage faith, the I'n-lon-schka was brought to the Osage by their cousins, the Kaw, and perhaps by the Ponca.

After the disruption of the move to Oklahoma and the preceding decades caused the loss of their traditional faith, the Osage were lost, spiritually. The performance of the mourning dance, in Gray Horse in 1911, is considered by many to be the last time one of the major ceremonies of the old religion was performed, and only the minor ceremonies, such as the naming ceremony, remained.

In 1884, however, the Kaw "brought back the drum," by introducing the Osage to the I'n-lon-schka. "Apparently they felt sorry for us because we didn't have any dances of our own, so they taught us the I'n-lon-schka," says Becky Johnson, an attorney of mixed Osage and Cherokee heritage. Other tribes have similar traditions, but few are as elaborate or as well maintained as those of the Osage and the Kaw.

Osage Funerals

The original Osage tradition for dealing with the dead involved not underground burial in a casket, an idea that horrified Osage of the day, but under a cairn of stones. The dead were placed in a sitting position against a large rock, often with a medicine bundle under them, and then stones were piled over them to form a mound. Early travelers record seeing these piles littering the countryside here and there at the turn of the century.

Eventually, pressure from religious leaders and the government led to a modification of the tradition, and today even traditional Osage are buried. The funeral ritual is still much the same, however. The body is laid out in the home for three days, during which time people stay up with the body. Meals are provided for funeral guests. The dead are buried in full Osage regalia, with an old-style lunch bucket packed with food, often meat pies or soup, but influenced by what the person liked in life. "She always tells me that when I die, she's going to make sure I get buried with a ham sandwich, a Diet Coke, and a pack of cigarettes," laughs one woman, speaking of an Osage friend. Many are buried with a small bundle of ritual medicine on their backs. When the person is laid to rest, a final meal is eaten, with prayers recited.

This cross hung with feathers demonstrates the way Christianity and Native religion have mixed on the Osage reservation.

Roughly translated, I'n-lon-schka means "playground of the eldest son" or "playground of the young man." The dance is seen as an opportunity for eldest sons to participate in an important religious event, although the whole tribe is involved in the festival. Though historians believe it originated as a dance of a warrior society, it had become a religious movement by the 1870s and incorporated more general spiritual themes.

The event takes place over three four-day weekends in June, running from Thursday to Sunday. It moves between the arbors of the three original settlements of the Osage nation in Oklahoma. On the first weekend, the dance is in Gray Horse, and the next weekend it moves to Hominy. The third weekend is spent resting and recovering, before moving to Pawhuska for the final four days of the festival. Each town has its own arbor, a large covered dance area surrounded by benches. Outside the arbor are the "camps," pavilions in which each group of dancers dress and prepare. Each family has its own bench it uses year after year, some plain, others painted in decorative colors.

At the center of the arbor is the drum, an incredibly sacred object that in many ways is the focus of the I'n-lon-schka. Around the drum is what is called "the committee," who plays the drum and leads the music for the dance. These men are highly respected members of the tribe, as well as accomplished musicians, and their leader is always someone who has dedicated his life to the study of the traditional music. "You could say he has a Ph.D. in Osage music," says Julie Lookout, referring to Scott George, who spent years learning at the side of her father, Morris Lookout, a respected leader of the committee. "The man who sits in that seat is like a great composer or conductor."

While it sounds strange to an outsider's ears, the drum is often referred to almost as if it is a person. If a member of the committee dies, the drum is said to "be in mourning." When a dancer makes a mistake, he must "pay the drum" to atone for it.

One of the most important roles in the I'n-lon-schka ceremony is that of

Francis LaFlesche and Osage Ritual and Song

Cultural anthropologist Francis LaFlesche (1857–1932), himself a member of the Omaha tribe, is responsible for much of what we know about traditional Osage rituals. Working together with two Osage, Black Dog and Saucy Calf, he succeeded in putting together detailed records of two important ceremonies, "The Songs of the Wa-xo'-be" and "The Rite of Chiefs," both associated with the Buffalo Bull Clan. He was fortunate to work when he did: ten years later there would be no one left who knew the ancient ceremonies; ten years earlier no one would have discussed them with an outsider.

LaFlesche dedicated much effort to recording the specific words of Osage chants and songs. The songs usually follow a rigidly structured, repetitive format and are heavy with images of animals and nature in their praise of Wa-kon-da, the Osage name for God.

Gift Giving Among the Osage

Giving gifts, particularly of food, is central to many Osage traditions. The I'n-lon-schka dance ceremony involves giving several thousands of dollars in gifts, food, and cash. Many other Osage ceremonies involve these elements, although generally on a smaller scale. Traditionally, when someone enters a house as a guest for the first time, the host is expected to give the guest a gift. One woman recalls an expensive dinner set her mother had: "We have a pitcher and one goblet—she gave the rest away over the years."

Meals accompany virtually every Osage ceremony, and there are expectations for people in certain roles to provide the groceries. Meals are often prepared by specific families who essentially have hereditary roles as cooks. The I'n-lon-schka, weddings, funerals, naming ceremonies, even the ritual for placing a first child on a cradleboard, all involve gifts of groceries and the preparation of a meal (sometimes in addition to other gifts). Sundays during the I'n-lon-schka are "the giveaways," when families give things to other families in exchange for things they've done for each other over the course of the year. Drummers are given blankets, cigarettes, and groceries. While the gift giving can become extravagant at times, most feel it evens out in the end, because everyone is both giving and receiving.

the Drum Keeper. The Drum Keeper is generally a young boy, an eldest son, and he is charged with keeping the drum between one I'n-lon-schka and the next. In reality, the responsibility falls on his whole family and involves more than simply taking care of the drum. Becoming Drum Keeper is an enormously expensive affair, one that some families would never be able to afford. The responsible family must not only keep the drum but also provide food for all the people at the festival (frequently many hundreds), as well as lodging for out-of-town guests and numerous gifts for important figures. The cost easily runs into many thousands of dollars. Still, it is an important role, and if they can afford it, people are anxious to have their sons chosen for it.

A person known as the whipman is in charge of making sure everything is done correctly and according to custom. Although certainly an important social occasion, the I'n-lon-schka is at its heart a very serious event, and it is important to the Osage that it be conducted with respect and in the proper manner. The tribe's own police force patrols the area around the arbor, with authority to remove anyone who is being rowdy, drunk, or disrespectful.

The ceremony at each town is much the same, although there are some differences unique to each place. The dancers are called at the beginning of each dance with the ringing of a bell, which summons them from their respective camps where they have been preparing. The first song is always what is called the "flag song," involving only the men. After that, the family songs are performed, and both men and women may dance. Women enter only after the men have circled the drum twice, and men dance toward the inside of the circle, while women move around the outside. Both men and women perform wearing only traditional Osage clothing, often ornately decorated with fingerweaving and beadwork, as well as colorful feathers and bells. Songs and prayers give thanks for family, for the blessings of the past year, and express hopes for another good year.

The final dance is the "tail dance." This dance features only one or two of the best dancers from each village. The music starts and stops suddenly, and the dancers freeze in place until the music resumes. Slowly the music builds until suddenly it stops and does not resume. This is the end of the ceremony. According to Morris Lookout, this buildup and abrupt ending is important. It lets the dance end at its peak excitement, and people leave with that intensity to carry them through the rest of the year until the next I'n-lon-schka.

The I'n-lon-schka has an important place in the heart of most Osage, regardless of their specific religious beliefs, and many who live far from the reservation come home for the festival. "I've traveled the world," said Julie Lookout, "but I always come back in June."

LORETTA M. HEWITT

ORIGINAL ALLOTTEE #2225

JUNE 30, 1907

JANUARY 1, 1999

BORN PAWHUSKA, OKLAHOMA

Gravestones indicate the connection between past and living clan members.

Chapter 5

Today's Social Structures

"We're all family," says Julie Lookout, "which doesn't mean we always get along." One does not have to talk to many people on the Osage Reservation before it becomes obvious that the Osage are one big family. Sometimes it seems that everyone you speak to is related to everyone else, somehow. This sense of relationship is something the Osage people value. It may be why so many who set off into the rest of the world find themselves drawn back to Osage County.

"There's just something about the land, and the people, that calls me back," says Robin Polhamus. She left Oklahoma in 1972 to study art in California, but after working there for a while, she returned home.

Traditionally, the basic social structure of the tribe was the clan. There were twenty-four Osage clans, each part of either the Sky People or the Earth People. Each clan was in turn further subdivided, and clan identity was inherited through the mother's line. Clans provided a number of important social functions: caring for less fortunate members, sharing food, and other responsibilities. Members of clans also shared particular *taboos*

Hominy School System provides support today to the Osage's social structures.

concerning their particular clan symbol. Clans provided a sort of social safety net in case misfortune befell a person, but they also served to give each person a specific role in the tribe—and in life.

Compared to many other tribes, the Osage have managed to maintain their clan identities fairly well. Most know at least whether they belong to the Sky People or the Earth People, and many know what clan or even sub-clan from which they are descended. There are still those that observe the tribal taboos. Robin Polhamus, for example, a member of the Thunder and Lightning clan, makes sure she wears metal in keeping with the traditions of her clan. Members of Sky People clans might avoid doing anything that pollutes the sky, such as burning trash.

Some clans, however, have died out entirely, and others have dwindled to only a few members. The Puma clan, for example, has only one surviving member at this time. In part because of this, and in part because of the disappearance of the ancient religion, clans have ceased to function as they once did, although family relationships remain vital to Osage society.

The village also remains an important social group, in some ways an adaptation of an older structure, the "band." While a number of towns are on the reservation, three have particular significance to the Osage: Pawhuska,

Hominy, and Gray Horse. These are the three original settlements the tribe formed when it first moved to the region in the 1870s, and they descend from the three bands that made up the Osage tribe at that time. The "Dwellers of the Upland Forest," the Little Osage, settled in Hominy, while the "Dwellers of the Thorny Thicket" built Pawhuska, and the "Dwellers Upon the Hilltop" who settled at Gray Horse were divisions of the Big Osage.

Each of the three original villages has an area known as "Indian Camp," the site of the original settlement where only the Osage may live, and its own dance arbor for the I'n-lon-schka. This yearly festival both bonds together members of the same villages and brings together the tribe as a whole. Those who do not actually live in one of the three villages, or "camps" as they are sometimes called, usually choose one of the three to affiliate themselves with for the purposes of the festival. The choice is made either through their ancestors' affiliations or because they feel a particular closeness to families from that village.

Dancers at the I'n-lon-schka arbor, as portrayed by Robin Polhamus.

Each family has their own place at the I'n-lon-schka camp.

Osage Clans

There were originally twenty-four Osage clans, or fireplaces, each divided between the Earth People and the Sky People. The clans did not have specific names, per se, but rather a series of life symbols, and the names used were merely references, direct or indirect, to those symbols. Each clan had its own specific ritual responsibilities and taboos to live by.

Below are the twenty-four clans as named by Francis LaFlesche. Keep in mind that there are many, many other names for these clans.

The Sky People

Elder Sky	Buffalo-Face	Gentle Sky
Wolf	Sun Carrier	Night
Last Sky	Men of Mystery	Buffalo Bull

The Earth People

Eagle	Bear	Puma
Metal Bunched	Elk	Crawfish
Wind	Elder Water	White Water
Gentle Ponca	Deer	Cattail
Clear the Way	Bow	Isolated Earth

The other distinction that becomes important at times is between those tribe members who have headrights (called "annuitants"), and those who do not. Because only those with headrights receive money for the oil and gas revenues, there tend to be financial gaps between these two groups, though in these days of relatively low tribal revenues, the difference is not as great as it once was. Still, this difference, coupled with the fact that those without headrights cannot vote or hold office in the tribal government, can lead to resentment between those with headrights and those without.

In a way, the Osage Nation as a whole functions as one large family or village. Ultimately it is a member's identity as Osage that triumphs over all other considerations. The members of the tribe have a bond in common, and that brings them together. Despite the disagreements that may occur in any family, the Osage still take care of their own.

Robin Polhamus is one of the best known Osage artists.

Chapter 6

Arts and Culture

The arts among the Osage reflect, in a way, the same changes evident in much of the society as a whole. The methods may be modern, the forms may be innovative, but somehow, underneath, the traditions and values of the ancient Osage tribe are mirrored. Sometimes this is obvious, at other times it is harder to see, but for those who have grown up Osage, the power of this culture somehow seems to be a part of everything they create.

One of the best known Osage artists is muralist and painter Robin Polhamus. Trained at Los Angeles Trade Tech through a grant from the Bureau of Indian Affairs, she graduated in 1974 with a degree in commercial art. Although she began her career doing commercial art such as signs and logos, much of her current work is focused on murals. Examples of her work can be found across the United States—from California to her home state of Oklahoma.

Much of Polhamus's recent work involves images significant to the Osage people. Her crowning achievements so far are a pair of enormous murals that grace the walls of the Tribal Council Chamber in Pawhuska. On one wall, a work called *It Has Been Said in This Lodge*, depicts the events of the Osage creation myth related earlier, from the descent of the Little Ones

Robin Polhamus says of her mural Osage One, *"Oil, gas, land and recording our history for future Osages is the reason I wanted to undertake this mural. I am truly honored to tell the story. . . ."*

from the Sky Lodge to the discovery of the Isolated Earth People and the young man's encounter with the spider. The work was inspired by John Joseph Mathews's book, *The Osage.*

On the opposite wall, a mural titled *Destiny to Dynasty* celebrates the past, present, and future of the Osage people, with images of important figures from Osage history, including members of the tribe and others who have helped the Osage people, such as oil pioneer Frank Phillips, founder of Phillips Petroleum and an honorary tribe member. Not only is the past displayed, but the future, too. Polhamus's painting also includes children, such as Blue Boy Starr, dressed in Indian clothing as though preparing for the I'n-lon-schka. "It's for them," says Polhamus, noting the children in the mural. "They are our future."

Although the paintings were done in the 1980s, they are not truly completed. She plans to continue to add significant individuals to the painting over time, making the mural, like the Osage tribe, a living, dynamic entity. Two people, Lynn McGuire and Buddy Red Corn, will be added soon.

Polhamus's cousin, Rosemary Wood, is also a noted artist, in addition to being a former councilwoman and a poet. (She also appears in the mural at the Council House.) Today she lives in the restored homestead on her father's original allotment.

Another well-known Osage artist is Wendy Ponca. Her art combines traditional elements with very modern methods using fabric. Her clothing designs include what she calls "ceremonial attire for the new millennium." This consists of dresses of draped Mylar, combined with body paint and eagle feathers, preserving the Osage tradition of beautiful and intricate ceremonial garb while creating a futuristic impression. Other works involve no clothing at all, as she continues to explore body painting, one of the oldest art forms. She served for over ten years as a professor of fiber arts and fashion design at the Institute of American Indian Arts in Santa Fe, New Mexico, and she holds a degree in art therapy.

Some traditional arts continue to flourish quietly. Rather than use beadwork, most Osage traditionally used fingerweaving to create colorful decorations for ceremonial gear or important objects, and the technique continues today. While only practiced by a handful of people, some Osage are making active efforts to teach the skill and preserve the art for another generation.

While the scrubby forests of Osage County provided little useful wood for building, the region's rocky ground was a perfect source of construction stone. Since the earliest days on the reservation, the Osage have had a

Destiny to Dynasty *by Robin Polhamus.*

Cha Tullis's art is inspired by Osage tradition.

reputation as masters of natural stone construction, an art evident in many of the buildings—both old and new—on the reservation. Today, a number of Osage serve in the construction and design of such buildings in Oklahoma and around the country.

Traditional Osage cooking also remains popular, though some elders complain that it has become more and more difficult to buy ingredients. "You can't buy the stuff for Native American food in the supermarket anymore," says Waltina Red Corn. "You can get foods from China or Thailand, but if you want to make Osage food, you just can't find it." Meat pies and fry bread are perhaps the most popular traditional treats, though not particularly healthy ones given their high grease content.

Of course, probably the greatest expression of Osage arts and culture is the I'n-lon-schka. It has meant the combination of traditional clothing, food, music, and dance, and it is the ultimate display of the ongoing importance of the arts to the tribe. The yearly festival is not only a religious ritual but also celebrates the continued richness and strength of Osage culture.

Osage Fingerweaving

Fingerweaving is among the oldest known arts of the North American Indians, and examples dating over 6,000 years old have been retrieved from a Florida peat bog. Unlike the Western tribes, who constructed large and complex looms for their weaving, Eastern tribes used fingerweaving with no more than a simple suspension loom. Before European contact, strands were spun from natural fibers like bark, milkweed silk, and soft strips of hide. After the arrival of the Europeans, most tribes switched to using wool. Osage weavers would sometimes unravel a small amount of yarn from trade blankets, spin it into thinner strings, and use it for fingerweaving.

Osage orange trees are a common sight on the Great Plains. The name of the tree comes from the Osage tribe. Although they are not true oranges, the fruit gives off an aromatic orangey scent.

Chapter 7

Contributions to the World

For most Americans, the word "ballet" probably does not trigger images of American Indians. It might surprise them, then, to know that one of the nation's greatest ballerinas ever, perhaps *the* greatest, was Osage.

Known to most as Maria Tallchief, among her people she was called *Wa-xthe-thomba*, "Woman Who Lives in Two Worlds." In a way, that is exactly what she did, living both in the ancient culture of her ancestors and in the cultured world of ballet as she performed in New York, Paris, and other great cities of the world.

Born in 1925 to Joseph Tall Chief, a full-blooded Osage, and a Scots-Irish mother, Maria grew up in Fairfax, Oklahoma. Her father had done quite well in the oil boom, and the family took frequent vacations to Colorado Springs to escape the Oklahoma heat. It was there, while staying at the Broadmoor Hotel, that young Maria took her first ballet lesson at the age of three. Both she and her mother fell in love with the idea.

Ballet lessons became a weekly affair by the time she was five years old, and soon her younger sister Marjorie joined her. Marjorie would become a famous ballerina in her own right. In 1933, the family moved to Los Angeles, and the girls continued training there. At the age of seventeen, Maria went to New York to audition.

She joined the Ballet Russe de Monte Carlo and soon became a featured soloist. Later, she became part of the New York City Ballet, where she danced from 1947 to 1960. Her 1949 performance of *Firebird* by George Ballanchine was the event that launched her onto the world stage. Critics the world over praised her work, and in 1953, President Dwight Eisenhower named her "Woman of the Year." That same year, the governor of Oklahoma honored her as well, highlighting her pride in her native heritage as an example for the many tribes in his state.

Maria and her sister Marjorie went on to found the Chicago City Ballet, and she served for a while as its artistic director. After her retirement from dancing, she directed and taught at a number of dance schools across the country. Through it all, she never lost touch with her Osage heritage, and she often commented on her love for the ceremonial dances of her tribe.

The Tallchief sisters are not alone in their contributions. The Osage tribe has given this world much, in many different fields. Some, like Maria and Marjorie Tallchief, made their mark in the arts, but others did so in politics or in war. This book cannot hope to name them all but merely highlights some examples of those Osage who have helped make this world what it is today.

While ballet is not an endeavor one usual connects with Oklahoma, Lynn McGuire made her mark in something much more commonly associated with the state—rodeo. She went to fourteen national finals, and in 1993, she became the only woman to ever qualify in the national finals for team roping. She was two-time world champion in steer roping, not to mention being named Miss Indian Rodeo as well.

While McGuire is easily the most prominent Osage in the sport, she is not alone. Osage County is almost as much cattle country as it is oil country, and many members of the tribe take part in the rodeo. Gole Maker, another Osage, was a rodeo champion in barrel racing. Barton Carter was the World Champion steer roper for ten years.

The Osage have also made their impact as educators, authors, and *activists*. Perhaps one of the best-known Osage figures is John Joseph Mathews. Known primarily as an author, he was also a naturalist, scholar, historian, and artist. His books brought the beauty of the prairie to the rest of the world as he explored life among the Osage in the 1930s and 1940s. His

Lynn McGuire is proud of her achievements. She and other Osage have contributed much to our world.

third book, *Talking to the Moon*, has been called "an Osage *Walden*"; it's a thoughtful look at both the people and wildlife of Osage country. Both his novels and historical works are dedicated to the preservation of Osage culture.

George "Tink" Tinker is an author and professor at the Iliff School of Theology in Denver. He has taught Native American culture and religion, as well as cross-cultural and Third World theological traditions. He is particularly interested in justice and peace studies, and has a reputation as an activist in the field of racial justice. His books include *Missionary Conquest: The Gospel and the Native American Genocide*. He serves as director of the Four Winds American Indian Survival Project in Denver and as an advisor to IMADR, the International Movement Against All Forms of Discrimination and Racism.

Another Osage activist works closer to home. Rose Mary Shaw fights domestic violence among Oklahoma's Native American population. Along with Jeannie Jones, a Chickasaw, she helped found the Oklahoma Native

American Coalition, which seeks to stop violence and abuse against women and children among twelve different tribes. She has endured threats and abuse in the course of her work.

One of the most important Osage figures in American history is Charles D. Curtis. Of mixed Osage and Kaw blood, he served in a number of positions over his four decades in the federal government. Trained as a lawyer, he spent fourteen years as representative from Kansas in the House before becoming the first Native American to be elected to the Senate. He served in the Senate for twenty years, five of them as the majority leader, where he authored the Indian Citizen Act of 1925. He is credited with paving the way for Oklahoma statehood. Although he failed to win the nomination for president, Curtis finished out his long and distinguished career as vice president under Herbert Hoover; Curtis was the only Native American to ever hold that position.

Possibly the biggest impact the Osage have made on the country is in war. During the World War I, the council set aside a 5,000-acre (2,025 hectares) tract as a Naval Oil Reserve, a tradition that has continued until today. The Osage have lived up to their ancient reputation as determined warriors and have served with distinction in many American wars.

Within hours of the attack on Pearl Harbor, Osage war drums sounded to call the warriors to battle. In 1943, according to one report, 381 Osages were serving in the U.S. military, and by the end of the conflict, 519 Osage had volunteered for service, about a third of those eligible. Twenty-six were killed in action. On the home front, two hundred Osage, including many women, helped to build airplanes in Tulsa. Still more tribe members were active in bond sales, scrap metal drives, and bandage rolling; the tribe itself paid for a training plane for use by the troops.

The most prominent Osage in World War II was Clarence Tinker. The first Native American to attain the rank of major general, he served in the Army Air Corps. In the buildup to war, he developed the plan used to secure the Panama Canal and Caribbean against German attack. Assuming responsibility for the defense of Hawaii following the raid on Pearl Harbor, Tinker led the attacks on Wake and Midway Islands. He was a pioneer in the field of modern air tactics and was a proponent of aggressive bombing. He died when his plane was shot down during the Battle of Midway, making him the first American general killed in combat during World War II.

Buddy Red Corn, now an employee of the Osage Nation, served with distinction during the Vietnam conflict. Acting as a mortar man, he was

The library at the White Hair Memorial allows Osage to research their family history.

Billy Ponca works at the White Hair Memorial to preserve her people's heritage.

Andrew Redcorn is proud he could serve America—and he is proud of his nation's history of service.

The Millionaire Company

World War I broke out in 1914 and lasted until 1919, although the United States did not truly join until its declaration of war against Germany in 1917. About 120 full-blooded Osage men and many mixed-bloods joined the military at this time. Many of these belonged to the 36th Division, Company E, comprised of the Texas and Oklahoma National Guards. This unit contained so many wealthy oilmen and ranchers, many of them Osage, that it was called the "Millionaire Company." According to a newspaper of the day: "Collectively, they owned many square miles of the richest oil and mineral lands of Oklahoma, and back home, there were thousands of dollars in royalties piling up every day for the buying of Liberty Bonds."

awarded the Army commendation medal with V-Device and with Oakleaf Cluster. His son, James "Dickens" Red Corn, carried on the martial tradition of his family and tribe by serving during Operation Desert Storm; he was named Soldier of the Year and received other numerous awards.

In all aspects of life, the Osage have made an impact on their nation and world. It seems clear that they will continue to do so in the future.

The Osage remember and preserve their past even as they enter the twenty-first century.

Chapter 8

Hopes and Challenges

In the course of their history, the Osage have gone from a fierce and dominant tribe to a people who desperately fought disease and starvation for survival. They have gone from the wealthiest people in the world to relative poverty. Life has not always been easy for the Osage, but they have survived.

Some members of the tribe, particularly the older ones, are concerned about what has been lost during these changes. Many of the traditions that once pervaded Osage life have disappeared, and as elders die, more and more of the Osage culture is lost. "There are so many things that are just gone now," says Waltina Red Corn. She and her husband Raymond are respected elders in Pawhuska. "There are lots of things neither Raymond nor I remember, and we're some of the oldest left. We saw them when we were young, but it didn't seem important then, and we didn't pay attention." She worries about what is in danger of being lost in even one generation.

"Like what you do when a new baby comes home," she says. "There's a whole set of things you're supposed to do, when you put it on the cradleboard, and no one does it any more. And where is it written down? I don't think it is." Although she admits there is much she and her husband do not

The cattle industry is a form of livelihood for many Osage.

know, she hopes to videotape this and other Osage traditions for future generations. The Red Corns have also been active in retelling the traditional stories, and they believe children will remember.

A few years ago, some might not have had so positive an outlook when it came to the Osage language. Today, estimates of the number of fluent, native speakers are as low as one or two. Experts predicted extinction for the language within a generation. But efforts by educators and the tribal museum have made long strides toward preventing that loss. Language classes are offered at the museum on a regular basis, and interest remains high. By preserving their original tongue, the Osage safeguard a doorway to their past.

Oil has played a central role in the Osage's past, so it is not surprising that it may figure prominently in their future as well. More than any other issue, the ongoing lawsuits against the U.S. government over oil and gas revenues dominate discussions of the future with many Osage.

The lawsuits involve the government's management of the tribe's mineral revenues. In 1997, the Osage demonstrated that the price they were being paid for their oil was $1.50 to $2.30 less per barrel than the price for which it was being sold, effectively shortchanging the tribe of millions of dollars. In addition, the tribe contends that a check of the Bureau of Indian Affairs' accounting practices showed gross mismanagement of funds belonging to the tribe; those funds were undercalculated by at least $2.5 billion.

"They said 'Trust us.' And we did," says Charles O. Tillman, a former principal chief who served from 1990 to 2002; under his administration the lawsuits were filed. "And that turned out to be disastrous, because there was not the management, or expertise, or accountability, to handle that vast operation."

Many Osage have high hopes that this decision will return some of the wealth to the tribe that has been lacking in the years since the collapse of the oil boom. Still, the lawsuits have been in progress for several years, and the process might drag on for many more years. Even then, there is no guarantee of the courts' final decision. Suing the government is a difficult task, and the case is a complex one, with far-reaching implications for the future of the government's relations not only with the Osage but also with all Native American nations. Even if the tribe is unsuccessful in these lawsuits, however, there is little doubt the Osage tribe will go on, and remain strong.

Oil will continue to play an important role in the Osage Nation.

Through changing times, the Osage maintain their connection to the land.

The Osage view of the cosmos has always been a forward-looking one. Just as the sun moves unceasingly from the east to the west, so do all things continue to move onward. Things may change, but they do not stagnate. On the surface, the Osage are a very different people than they were a few hundred years ago. The world around them changed, and it changed them. "They wanted to make us into English-speaking, God-fearing farmers," says Brite Starr, an Osage educator. But while times may have changed what the Osage do, they have not changed who they are, a proud and strong people.

Further Reading

Callahan, Alice Anne. *The Osage Ceremonial Dance I'n-Lon-Schka*. Norman: University of Oklahoma Press, 1993.

Dorsey, George. *Traditions of the Osage*. New York: AMS Press, 2004.

Riehecky, Janet. *The Osage*. Mankato, Minn.: Bridgestone, 2003.

Vavra, Stephanie. *Who Really Saved Laura Ingalls?* New York: Quillwork, 2001.

Wolferman, Kristie C. *The Osage in Missouri*. Colombia: University of Missouri, 1997.

For More Information

Native American culture

falcon.jmu.edu/ ~ ramseyil/native.htm
www.hanksville.org/NAresources/

Osage Culture and History

www.missouri-history.itgo.com
www.osageindians.com
www.osagetribe.com
www.uark.edu

Publisher's Note:

The Web sites listed on this page were active at the time of publication. The publisher is not responsible for Web sites that have changed their address or discontinued operation since the date of publication. The publisher will review and update the Web sites upon each reprint.

Glossary

activists: People who do things in support of a cause.

allotments: Plots of land given to an individual or group of people.

archaeology: The scientific study of the remains of human life and activity.

boomtowns: Towns that enjoy a surge in business and population growth.

ceded: Yielded or granted, usually as the result of a treaty.

charter: A written document that creates and defines the franchises of a city, educational institution, or corporation.

cholera: An acute disease caused by a bacteria and characterized by severe gastrointestinal distress and diarrhea.

colonial: Something relating to or characteristic of a colony, especially one of the original thirteen American colonies.

Confederacy: The eleven Southern states that dropped out of the United States in 1860 and 1861.

contentious: Something likely to cause arguments.

constitution: The basic principles and laws of a nation, state, or social organization.

criteria: Standards on which decisions or judgments are made.

diverse: Having different characteristics.

embargo: A governmental order prohibiting the departure of commercial ships from its ports.

entrepreneurs: Those who organize, manage, and assume the risks of a business.

epidemics: Diseases affecting a large number of people at the same time.

fast: A period of going without food and sometimes also without drink, often done for religious reasons.

frontier: An area that forms the border between unsettled and developed territory.

Great Depression: A period of low economic activity and high levels of unemployment that occurred in the United States between 1929 and 1939.

guerilla: A person who commits irregular warfare, for example, harassment.

hallucinogenic: A substance that causes one to suffer from hallucinations (seeing of things that are not there).

hunter–gatherers: Members of a society in which food is obtained through hunting, fishing, and foraging rather than by farming.

Jesuit: A member of the Roman Catholic Society of Jesus, a religious order of monks who focused on education and missionary work.

lineal descendents: Heredity based on the direct male or female line of ancestors.

myth: A story that expresses or symbolizes a people's view of the world and their place in it.

nominally: Having to do with something that exists in name only.

patented: Legal privilege to use public lands.

posse: A large group of people temporarily organized to conduct a search.

precedent: Something that may serve as an example to authorize or justify something else.

Prohibition: The period in early twentieth-century American history when the manufacture, transportation, or sale of alcoholic beverages was forbidden except for medicinal or religious purposes.

referendum: The practice of putting to a popular vote a measure passed on or proposed by a legislative body or popular initiative.

repealed: Rescinded by authoritative action.

reservation: An area of land set aside for use by Native Americans.

royalties: Shares of profit retained by the grantor of a lease.

sacrament: Something tangible that carries spiritual meaning.

skepticism: An attitude of doubt or suspicion.

smallpox: A contagious disease characterized by skin eruptions and scarring.

sovereignty: The right to self-rule, self-govern.

speculators: People who assume a business risk with the hope of making a gain.

Sun Dance: A spiritual rite performed by Native Americans.

taboos: Things that are forbidden.

tuberculosis: A highly contagious, lung disease.

Union: The group of states that remained part of the federal United States during the Civil War.

vigilante: A self-appointed crime fighter.

vigils: The days of watching and waiting before a religious feast.

Index

Biographies

Philip Stewart was born in western New York State and raised near the Seneca Indian reservations there, where he developed an early interest in Native American culture. After graduating from the nearby Alfred University, he worked for several years at Cornell University, before moving to Fayetteville, Arkansas, to attend graduate school at the University of Arkansas. He lives there with his wife Cynthia and daughter Zea.

Martha McCollough received her bachelor's and master's degrees in anthropology at the University of Alaska-Fairbanks, and she now teaches at the University of Nebraska. Her areas of study are contemporary Native American issues, ethnohistory, and the political and economic issues that surround encounters between North American Indians and Euroamericans.

Benjamin Stewart, a graduate of Alfred University, is a freelance photographer and graphic artist. He traveled across North America to take the photographs included in this series.